HANNAH

A month in the presence of the mother of Samuel

CLAIRE
BENTON
EVANS

kevin
mayhew

kevin
mayhew

First published in Great Britain in 2019 by Kevin Mayhew Ltd
Buxhall, Stowmarket, Suffolk IP14 3BW
Tel: +44 (0) 1449 737978 Fax: +44 (0) 1449 737834
E-mail: info@kevinmayhew.com

www.kevinmayhew.com

9 8 7 6 5 4 3 2 1 0

ISBN 978 1 84867 977 1
Catalogue No. 1501599

Cover design by Rob Mortonson
© Image used under licence from Shutterstock Inc.
Edited by Linda Ottewell
Typeset by Angela Selfe

Printed and bound in Great Britain

Contents

About the author

Claire Benton-Evans has written extensively for Kevin Mayhew. Her work includes worship resources for all ages, such as the popular *All-Sorts Worship* series and *All-Sorts Prayer*. She is the author of *Beastly Bible Stories*, an eight book series that invites children to explore the Bible's library of weird, wonderful and extraordinary stories. Claire lives in Scotland and works as the Youth and Children Officer for the Diocese of Edinburgh in the Scottish Episcopal Church. She is a member of the Provincial Youth Committee and is a leader of the Scottish Episcopal Church's annual Youth Week. She is married with three children and enjoys theatre, wild swimming and hillwalking.

Introduction

Hannah might seem to us impossibly remote: a woman in a desert town who lived three thousand years ago and as many miles away; a second wife who longed for a son and then – extraordinarily – gave him away. But the Bible doesn't let us keep our distance. Like a reality TV show's all-seeing camera, the Bible connects us intimately with Hannah, showing us her tears and the tensions at home. It lets us eavesdrop on her conversations with her husband and her desperate prayers. It captures every word of this faithful woman's spontaneous song of praise.

Hannah's life is contained in just 49 verses of the Old Testament, yet 19 of these feature her direct speech. For almost half of her brief time in the spotlight, the Bible allows Hannah to speak for herself! This gives her story an unusual power and immediacy.

The 30 meditations in this book encourage you to spend a month in Hannah's company, finding some perhaps surprising common ground. Each day links an aspect of Hannah's story with a Bible reading, which is accompanied by a short reflection and a prayer. The reflections make imaginative connections between today's world and Hannah's, by way of Netflix, art, Facebook, poetry, YouTube, musical theatre and more. I hope that connections like these will help you to integrate your faith and Bible study with the real life you're living today.

This book is for everyone, not only for women or for those who have children. The meditations will explore such diverse matters as God's generosity and how we might 'pay it forward', how much of our lives we dedicate to God, and what it might mean if we really were to 'go in peace'. We will consider, among other things, the impact of bullying and emotional abuse, the challenge of speaking out against powerful people and the support of fostering and adoptive families in our churches.

It is said that we can't really know a person until we have walked a mile in their shoes: why not spend a month walking in Hannah's faithful footsteps, to see where she and God might lead you?

1
Blessed is the fruit

The Handmaid's Tale has been a TV sensation. Based on Margaret Atwood's novel, it depicts a horrifying world in which infertility threatens the future of humanity. A totalitarian government bans women from the workplace and takes away their rights to own property or bank accounts. High status couples who cannot have children are given a fertile 'handmaid' to conceive a child for them. Women in this society are controlled and defined by their ability to have children.

Read 1 Samuel 1:1, 2.

Hannah's story begins as many in the Bible do, with a list of fathers and sons, naming the generations as if women had had nothing to do with this family tree. When at last two women are mentioned, the only things we learn about them are their marital and childbearing status. What must it have been like to be a wife in this patriarchal society? She could not choose to remain child-free: childlessness was seen as a disgrace and a sign of God's punishment. Imagine the weight of expectation upon you to become the mother of many sons (and daughters). Imagine what it was like to be childless Hannah and fertile Peninnah; reflect on how Elkanah's family may have compared the two women.

Talk to God about the comparisons we make between women, or perhaps between ourselves and others, based on whether or not they have children. Ask God gently to shine a light on any hidden assumptions you may have.

Prayer

Father, forgive us for how we have judged ourselves and others. Free us to be ourselves in your eyes, and to share that freedom with other people.

2

An unhappy beginning

The popular musical *Blood Brothers* starts with a gunshot. The curtain opens on a dead man, and a mother grieving over the body of her murdered son. The story then unfolds from the beginning, before the boy's birth, but we always know how it's going to end.

Read Genesis 17:15-22.

Childless women have a special place in the story of God's covenant with his people. 90-year-old Sarah became the 'mother of nations', then barren Rebekah became the mother of Jacob, the patriarch; Jacob's own infertile wife, Rachel, eventually bore two founding fathers of the 12 tribes of Israel. Much later, of course, Christianity's own story began with the children of Mary the virgin and elderly Elizabeth. In this context, when we are introduced to childless Hannah, we already suspect that we know the end of her story: she will give birth to a God-given child who will have a special place in the history of God's people.

These familiar, ancient stories can impose their patterns on us today. I wonder how many childless women have felt that if they were faithful enough, if they just prayed hard enough, then God would give them a child? In reality, not every childless couple's prayers will be answered by a special pregnancy. If you are close to someone in this situation, consider how you might walk faithfully with them as their own story unfolds, without presuming to know the ending.

Prayer

Father, we pray for all those longing for a child of their own; for men and women undergoing tests and fertility treatment. You know how you will answer our prayers – help us to trust in you.

3

The patter of tiny feet

It's 1920. A childless couple move from their home town to start a new life farming a remote homestead in the Alaskan wilderness. In *The Snow Child* by Eowyn Ivey, the wife's motivation is clear from the start: she is running away from the sound of all her nephews, nieces and neighbours' children. The patter of their tiny feet has been a constant, saddening reminder of what she sees as her own failure to have children, so she seeks refuge in the snowy silence of Alaska.

Read 1 Samuel 1:3, 4.

Walking cross country to the temple at Shiloh would have been quite a family outing. The distance is around 17 miles as the crow flies, but this is hot, dry hill country. I wouldn't like to be in Peninnah's shoes, taking 'all her sons and daughters' on such a hike: imagine the choruses of 'Mummy, my feet hurt!' and 'Are we nearly there yet?' Like many parents, she must have rolled her eyes at the incessant and exhausting demands of her offspring, with little thought for those, like Hannah, who long for children of their own.

Consider those in your church congregation for whom the sound of small children is a reminder of pain and regret. What can you do to support and include them, especially on Mothering Sunday, at baptisms, in family services and at the Christmas crib service?

Prayer

Lord, help me to be sensitive to the feelings of those without children. Help me to listen without judgement, offer support without presumption and love without limit.

4

Best Beloved

How do I love thee? Let me count the ways.
I love thee to the depth and breadth and height
My soul can reach . . . I love thee with the breath,
Smiles, tears, of all my life.

(From Sonnets from the Portuguese 43 by Elizabeth Barrett Browning)

This famous expression of a woman's love for her husband was written over 175 years ago but has lost none of its power. Older by far is the astonishingly passionate Song of Songs, which features in many wedding services.

Read Song of Songs 8:6, 7.

Elkanah loved his wife Hannah best, in spite of her inability to bear children. In a religious society which understood children to be a sign of God's blessing, and in a marriage shared with a very fertile wife, how strong must that love have been! As we consider Hannah's story over the coming days, notice the ways in which her husband shows his love for her. In 1 Samuel 1:4, 5 we see that he regularly gives her gifts: an extra portion of the choice meat he offers for sacrifice. It's a loving gesture we still use today, when we give our loved one an extra helping at dinner, or that last slice of cake.

Prayer

Thank God for married love which binds people together. Praise him for the strong marriages you know and for the resilient love that 'bears all things, believes all things, hopes all things, endures all things'. Ask God to help those whose marriages are struggling, often in ways that no one else sees.

5

Bullied

The work of the NSPCC, Childline and other charities in recent years has done a great deal to support and inform children who are being bullied. When I was a child, I had a notion that bullying was something that boys did to each other, involving fists and stolen dinner money. It took me years to realise that the way some children in my class treated others – belittling them or excluding them – was also a form of bullying. It's hard to ignore being ignored, and it's harder still to stand up to verbal abuse: the constant struggle can have a real impact on a child's emotional and even physical well-being.

Read 1 Samuel 1:4-7.

This is one of those moments in Hannah's story that is as intimate as a hidden camera in a reality TV show, which captures the sideways glance, the whispered insult and the sly taunts between rivals on *Love Island* or in the *Big Brother* house. Hannah is suffering what we would now describe as emotional bullying at the hands of her husband's other wife, described in most translations as her 'rival'. Imagine yourself in Hannah's place. In what ways are the two wives rivals? When does the bullying happen? How does it feel? How long does the bullying continue? In Hannah's place, how might you respond?

Does this part of Hannah's story remind you of an experience of bullying? Talk to God about it, whether you have experienced bullying yourself or are worried about others, whether the bullying is in childhood or adulthood.

Prayer

Lord, may you comfort and strengthen the victims of bullying; may you intervene and change the hearts of the bullies themselves.

6

Foot-in-mouth disease

Miss Bates is a good-hearted but dull chatterbox; Emma is a witty, beautiful young woman. At a picnic for friends and neighbours, an equally witty young man proposes a silly game: everyone should say either one very clever thing, two quite clever things or three very boring things. Miss Bates says self-deprecatingly that the third option should be easy for her. Emma quips, 'Ah! ma'am, but there may be a difficulty. Pardon me, but you will be limited as to number – only three at once.' As readers of Jane Austen's *Emma*, we cringe with the heroine as she opens her mouth to be amusing, and realises too late that she has said something deeply hurtful to Miss Bates.

Read Elkanah's attempt to comfort his childless wife in 1 Samuel 1:8.

Why does Elkanah ask these questions? How is he feeling? How might these questions make Hannah feel? Elkanah intends to buck Hannah up (as if to say, 'Well, you've still got me!'), but in fact he sounds as if he's reproaching her for feeling sad about her childlessness ('Aren't I enough for you?') We have all had the experience of speaking before we have fully weighed the likely impact of our words: we open our mouth and put our foot in it. The memory can still make us sorry or ashamed, years later.

Prayer

Father, forgive us for all the times our words have caused pain to others deliberately, thoughtlessly or unintentionally. Help us to make amends if we can; help us to weigh our words more carefully in future.

7

The Presence

'The Presence' is a painting that hangs in St Mary's Episcopal Cathedral in Edinburgh. In the background, the Eucharist is being celebrated at the brightly-lit High Altar, but the painting is dominated by the shadowy, empty nave – empty apart from two figures in the dark foreground, furthest away from the altar. Behind the back pew, almost creeping behind a pillar, is a woman in black who is kneeling or collapsing in distress. Approaching her is the radiant figure of Christ, his hand raised in blessing. The distraught woman is just turning her pale face towards him.

Read 1 Samuel 1:9, 10.

I imagine 'The Presence' when I think of Hannah's desperate prayer. How dark and empty her future seemed! All she could do was take her tears, her heartache and her prayers to God – and we know that he heard her.

Have you, like Hannah, prayed alone in an empty church, when you couldn't think what else to do? Remember yourself there: looking back, where was God? How did he respond? If you, like Eli, were to come across someone alone and in distress in your church, how would you respond? Has this ever happened to you? What did you say or do?

Prayer

Father, comfort all those who seek your presence today where no one but you can see their tears. May all our churches be spaces where those who seek may find you. Help us minister to the Hannahs we meet in our own place of worship.

8

Bargaining with God

Dear God,

Please make my cat get better. If you do I promise I will be good.

Dear God,

If you can fix it so that I am good at maths I will keep my bedroom tidy for a year.

Amen.

Straightforward, specific prayers like these will be familiar to anyone who has had the privilege of praying with children. It's the kind of simple proposition many of us learnt from our parents: '*If* you're good, *then* we will let you stay up late.' No wonder children's prayers sometimes bargain with God in this way!

Bargaining is something we do as adults, too. The 'stages of grief' were described by the psychiatrist Elisabeth Kübler-Ross, in an attempt to chart the emotional journey of people diagnosed with a terminal disease. They are: denial, anger, bargaining, depression and acceptance. These stages are experienced by people dealing with bereavement and many different kinds of loss. For people of faith, it can be tempting to bargain with God, as Hannah does.

Read Hannah's prayer: 1 Samuel 1:11.

Imagine yourself in Hannah's place, praying these words. What do you think of her prayer? Why do you think God answered her? Have you ever said to God, 'If you . . . then I will . . .'?

Prayer

Talk to God about the temptation to bargain with him when we are in despair. Pray for all those people, unknown to you but known to God, who are bargaining in prayer for specific outcomes. Pray for them to know God's love, especially when the answer to their prayer is not what they bargained for.

9
Special

When Sarah sees a stranger who looks just like her jump in front of a train, she embarks on a long and dangerous journey to find out who this mysterious twin was. Over several seasons of the TV drama *Orphan Black*, she discovers more women like her and together they unearth the truth: a shadowy scientific corporation created them all as clones. Their very DNA contains a sequence which is a barcode, marking them out as the property of the corporation that made them.

Read Numbers 6:1-8.

Becoming a Nazirite meant being separate, special and 'holy to the Lord'. Men and women could make the Nazirite vow, and mothers could do so on behalf of their children. You may remember that the mother of Samson was instructed by an angel to make this vow: she was another childless woman who bore a special son. Before Hannah's longed-for baby has even been conceived, she vows that he will be a Nazirite. His special status will be knitted into his DNA, like a barcode that says: 'This child belongs to God.'

Think about how much of yourself you dedicate to God. How do you mark out something in your life as special and 'holy to the Lord'? Think about your time, energy, work, relationships… What more might you give?

Prayer

Lord, everything I have comes from you. Help me to remember this with gratitude, and show me how to set aside something that is just for you.

10

Misunderstood

It's easy to get swept away by the wonderful story of Pentecost: such drama! Wind, fire and miraculous speaking in tongues – what better origin story for the Church? Yet in the middle of the Pentecost account there is a discordant note. The people on the streets are amazed, yes, but also confused – and some are downright cynical about the inspired disciples: 'They must be drunk!' they sneer, loudly enough for Peter to hear above the noise of the crowd.

Read 1 Samuel 1:12-14 and compare it with Acts 2:1-15.

Hannah and the disciples are not the only people of faith to be so misunderstood, before or since. Genuine religious fervour has often been dismissed as drunkenness, derided as folly or (these days) regarded as a sign of psychological disturbance. Remember that Jesus gave specific instructions about this to his disciples: 'Blessed are you when people revile you and persecute you and utter all kinds of evil against you falsely on my account. Rejoice and be glad, for your reward is great in heaven, for in the same way they persecuted the prophets who were before you' (Matthew 5:11, 12).

Have you ever been insulted, belittled or attacked because of your faith? Have you seen it happen to others, either in person or online? How did it make you feel? What was your response?

Prayer

Pray for all those whose faith is misunderstood and mocked; pray for those who feel isolated by their faith from their family, friends or co-workers. Pray especially for Christians across the world who are persecuted, tortured and killed for their faith.

11

Speaking out

Emma Gonzalez was a student at the school in Parkland, Florida, where 17 people died in a mass shooting. Her powerful speech at an anti-gun rally caught the attention of the world's media. She spoke against President Trump and the gun lobby; in a strong voice which was charged with emotion she called for her schoolmates' deaths to mark the end of mass shootings. You can watch her speech on YouTube: imagine the courage it took for this young woman to stand up to powerful forces, and to speak out while still struggling with her own grief.

When Hannah was grief-stricken, Eli the priest accused her of being drunk, and tried to shoo her away from the temple.

Read her response in 1 Samuel 1:15, 16.

This is a powerful riposte from a woman in despair. First of all, she contradicts Eli – 'No,' my lord' – and does so with a deference that undermines his accusation that she is out of control. Then she is frank about her feelings. She emphatically argues that she is sober, and states: 'I have been pouring out my soul before the Lord.' It's as if she is planting her feet firmly on holy ground. Again she respectfully contradicts the priest's view of her: 'Do not regard your servant as a worthless woman.' Finally she emphasises her 'great anxiety and vexation'. Hannah's uninterrupted speech completely changes Eli's attitude towards her, as we shall see in tomorrow's reading.

Prayer

Pray for those who speak up and speak out to change people's hearts and minds. Pray for those in public life who 'hunger and thirst for righteousness'; pray for those who in their work or private lives try to speak out and make a difference.

12
Intercession

In some churches, power seems to rest with those who compile the rotas. One such was the elderly lady who did the Prayer Rota. She had been part of the church for years and liked to feel she knew everyone and everything. As she ran her sharp eyes over that week's intercessions, she spotted some unfamiliar names amongst those for whom prayer was being offered. 'But who are these people?' she demanded to know. 'Why are we praying for them?'

When Hannah prayed in the temple, she explained to the priest that she was 'deeply troubled' and was praying with 'great anxiety and vexation', but she did not explain the cause of these feelings, and from the evidence we have, Eli did not ask.

Read Eli's response to Hannah in 1 Samuel 1:17.

It is enough for Eli to know that Hannah needs help, and he simply asks God to grant her prayer. This is the true meaning of *intercession*: when we pray for others in our churches on a Sunday morning, we are simply intervening on other people's behalf and praying for them. Think about the intercessions in your church. Do you know everyone who is mentioned? Does it matter? Does it help to know exactly why you are praying for them, or is it enough to trust that God already knows their needs?

Prayer

Father, we pray for those whose needs are known to us, and those whose needs are known only to you.

13

Go in peace

The United Nations International Day of Peace is held on 21 September each year. It began as a call for ceasefires across the world's conflict zones; now it is a day devoted to the larger goal of building a peaceful world. The UN recognised that this would not be possible unless action were taken to improve social and economic justice and human rights for people everywhere, so the member states adopted 17 Sustainable Development Goals to tackle key issues including poverty, gender equality and climate change.

In the Bible, peace is more than the absence of war. Peace is a God-given state of justice and order, when right relationships are restored between people and nations. This is the kind of peace promised by the 'Prince of Peace' (Isaiah 9:6).

Read 1 Samuel 1:17-19.

What evidence is there here that Hannah did indeed 'go in peace'? What immediate difference did Eli's blessing make to her and her relationships? Think about those times when you have felt God's peace in your life. What difference did it make? Think about the words that we regularly hear after Holy Communion: 'Go in peace to love and serve the Lord.' What does this mean to you? If we really 'go in peace', how might this change us?

Prayer

Lord, we pray for peace in our hearts that only you can give, for peace in our own lives, and for our part in bringing about a peaceful world.

14

God remembered

The Earth, say'st thou? The Human race?
By Me created? Sad its lot?
Nay: I have no remembrance of such place:
such world I fashioned not.

In his poem, *God-forgotten*, Thomas Hardy gives voice to his agnostic fears. He dreams that these words are spoken by God, who at last dimly remembers the 'tainted ball' he created aeons ago.

Read 1 Samuel 1:19, 20 and compare it with Genesis 30:22-24.

When God answered these women's prayers, the Bible uses the expression 'God remembered her.' It is hard for some readers not to wonder whether he had previously 'forgotten' her. Certainly that must have been how it felt for Hannah and Rachel, especially in those days long before the tests, investigations and treatments of fertility clinics could give some insight into the causes of their childlessness.

We know that our loving Creator cannot forget us. Jesus said: 'Are not five sparrows sold for two pennies? Yet not one of them is forgotten in God's sight. But even the hairs of your head are all counted. Do not be afraid; you are of more value than many sparrows' (Luke 12:6, 7). God knows us and loves us, but because we are only human we sometimes forget this. Have you ever felt that God has forgotten you or someone close to you? When have you felt that he 'remembered' you?

Prayer

Father, we pray for all those who in their sadness feel that you have forgotten them. May they know your love in their hearts and feel your presence with them. May they know that you always remember them.

15

What's in a name?

Among the many extraordinary things in *The Hitchhiker's Guide to the Galaxy* by Douglas Adams, we read the first thoughts of a whale that has suddenly popped into existence miles above an alien planet. As it plummets, the doomed whale spends its few moments of life naming things – including the big, flat, hard surface that is fast approaching.

In the Genesis account of creation, naming was Adam's first act, too:

Read Genesis 2:19, 20.

Naming is an act of authority: Adam named the creatures God had given him, just as new parents decide their baby's name. In the Bible, God is the giver of significant names. He renamed Abram and Sarai as Abraham and Sarah, the father and mother of his people. He called Jacob 'Israel' – the one who fought with God. Later, God's messenger named Jesus (in Hebrew, Yeshua or Joshua, meaning 'God saves') and then Jesus himself had the authority to name Simon as Peter, 'the rock' on which the Church would be built. So in 1 Samuel 20, it's unusual that Hannah claims the authority to give her son a significant name: Samuel, which means 'asked for' – he is God's answer to prayer.

Think about what your own name means. Do you like your name's meaning or find it significant? Are there other names you prefer or dislike being called?

Prayer

Father, you know each of us inside out. Bless those who feel that their name does not reflect the real person inside. Comfort those who feel judged by the names others call them.

16

The Unbreakable Vow

In *Harry Potter and the Half-Blood Prince,* the Unbreakable Vow is a potent spell which binds two wizards together in a promise. If either party breaks the Vow, they will die.

In the Old Testament, vows were not always so unbreakable. Leviticus Chapter 27 explains how vows can be exchanged for donations of money to the temple priests: there is a sliding scale, depending on whether it is a person, an animal or land that has been promised to the Lord. Husbands also had the final say over vows made by their wives: 'Any vow or any binding oath to deny herself, her husband may allow to stand, or her husband may nullify' (Numbers 30:13). If a husband overrules his wife's vow, 'the Lord will forgive her' (verse12).

Read 1 Samuel 1:21-23.

Jewish law gave both Hannah and Elkanah an honourable way out of her vow. Yet, having cradled their firstborn son in her arms, Hannah stands by her promise to give him to God 'for all time'. Perhaps even more surprisingly, Elkanah respects her decision, submitting himself humbly to God's will. What do you think made Hannah decide to keep her promise? What might Elkanah have thought when he first heard of his wife's vow? What do you think made him support her decision?

Think about the promises you have made in your life, and to whom you have made them. Which ones have been easy to keep? Which ones have you struggled with? Which ones have you broken?

Prayer

Father, help us to make promises wisely. Forgive us and heal us when we break them and help us to keep the promises that matter.

17
Weaning

I breastfed my three children and I remember it as a very happy, if intense, experience. The physical bond between us was a daily wonder to me: everything I ate was fuel for making milk, and if my baby suddenly put on a growth spurt and fed particularly greedily, I'd eat two dinners and still want more. It was a constant connection which meant I couldn't physically be away from my baby for more than a few hours at a time, but it only lasted a few months and I wouldn't have changed it for the world.

In the UK today, babies begin to be weaned onto solid food between four and six months old. Most children are fully weaned by the time they are a year old. Yet in many ancient cultures, such as the Inuit of the Canadian Arctic, mothers breastfed their children until they became pregnant with their next child: this might be after three or even five years. This was likely the case in Old Testament times, too. So Samuel may have been four when Hannah weaned him – about the age that British children start nursery, and begin to learn how to manage short-term separation from their parents.

Read 1 Samuel 1:24-28.

Can you imagine yourself in Hannah's shoes? What might it have been like for young Samuel? Imagine how Elkanah felt, too. Is there a family close to you who is dealing with separation?

Prayer

Father, we pray for the bond between parents and children, and especially for those families who are separated against their will. We pray for divorcing families, for children taken into care, for refugee families and for parents and children divided by poverty.

18

Empty nest

As I write, my eldest child is packing for the third year of her university course, which she will spend in France. Her brother is currently working in Canada and looking to extend his stay: we are discussing with him, via Skype, the intricacies of work permits. As parents do, we are wondering how these children of ours grew up so fast and, while we miss having them around, we rejoice to see them spreading their wings and finding their own way in life.

Read Psalm 127.

Sit with the image of children 'like arrows in the hand of a warrior'. A warrior's arrows are vital for his armoury, certainly, but what use are they if he keeps them permanently gathered up in his quiver? An arrow is meant to fly from the bow and find its target: that's what it's *for*. The truth is, none of us gets to keep our children. From the moment they are born, they are growing up and away from us. Hannah took her young son to the temple and 'left him there for the Lord'. (1 Samuel 1:28). Her action may seem incomprehensible to us, but it is simply an accelerated version of what all parents have to do in the end: give our children away.

Think about the challenges of children leaving home. How might you and your church reach out to parents suffering from 'empty nest syndrome'?

Prayer

Father, you understand what it is like to give up your Son. Guide all parents as they give their growing children more independence; comfort those who grieve over their empty bedrooms; strengthen family relationships as parents and children move away from each other.

19

Magnificat

When I speak to churches about the spirituality of children, I like to ask them this question: who was the first person to worship Jesus as the Son of God? Everyone thinks for a bit, then makes suggestions. A shepherd? A wise man? His parents? No. According to Luke's Gospel, the first person to worship Jesus was an unborn child – John the Baptist. His pregnant mother, Elizabeth, tells Mary: 'As soon as I heard the sound of your greeting, the child in my womb leapt for joy' (Luke 1:44). Like a spark lighting a fire, John's spontaneous act of joyful recognition ignites Mary's praise.

Read Luke 1:46-55.

Mary's song of praise, known as the Magnificat, is very well known to Christians. It may be heard nightly wherever Evensong is said or sung; churches usually read it during Advent. If you could keep just one verse from it, what would it be and why? Mary knew her Scripture, and would have been familiar with Hannah's song of praise, which we will be considering over the coming days. As we look at Hannah's words, notice the ways in which they are echoed by Mary, and the ways in which the two songs differ.

Have you ever felt an irresistible urge to praise God? What prompted you? Take some time to think about how you felt, and what you said and did to praise him.

Prayer

Lord, open our eyes to recognise your presence in the world. Like John, may we worship you in what we do. Lift up our hearts in gratitude and let us praise you as Mary did.

20

War zone

Over recent years, attitudes to domestic violence and abuse have begun to change. Violent incidents in the home often used to be trivialised by police as 'just a domestic', and isolated women were left to manage abusive partners as best they could. Now domestic abuse in all its forms – including emotional abuse and coercive control – is being recognised for what it is: an ongoing war within the home, whose victims are usually women and children.

Read 1 Samuel 2:1-5.

Notice the references to war and weapons in Hannah's speech. Remember, these words are spoken by a wife whose life has been confined to the domestic sphere. When has she had to put on armour or face a mighty enemy with bow and arrows? Where do these fierce images spring from? What battles has she known?

Hannah's pain at her own childlessness was made worse by the emotional abuse inflicted by her husband's second wife. Have you or someone close to you experienced an abusive relationship? Are you worried about a current situation? Talk to God about it, and also consider asking someone you trust for help.

Prayer

Father, we pray for all those who are struggling privately in an abusive relationship. Find them a way to be free and whole again; show us how best to help. Transform the hearts and minds of their abusers.

21

Topsy-turvy

On a wet afternoon in the Lake District, I took my son to a place which promised all sorts of optical illusions. I thought these would be visual puzzles: what I didn't expect was the immersive experience of walking around topsy-turvy rooms. Ceilings became floors, taps dripped uphill and balls on a sloping billiard table rolled upwards. My son leant easily off a wall ladder at an angle of 45 degrees; in a room with a chequered floor, he looked as tiny as a toddler in one corner and like a giant in the other. I was wholly disorientated – indeed, signs warned pregnant visitors that there was a risk of losing your balance in these rooms. The place seemed to turn the world upside down.

Read Psalm 113 and compare it with 1 Samuel 2:6-8.

Throughout the Bible we encounter this vision of a world set to rights by being turned upside down – the mighty are cast down while the poor and lowly are raised up. It's what Jesus promised in his Sermon on the Mount: 'Blessed are the poor in spirit, for theirs is the kingdom of heaven. Blessed are those who mourn, for they will be comforted. Blessed are the meek, for they will inherit the earth' (Matthew 5:3-5).

Think back to when your life has been turned upside down. Was this transformation for the better, or not? Where did you see God at work in it?

Prayer

Lord, may your love turn lives upside down. Set to rights those whose lives are going the wrong way.

22
Prophecy

You may know *An Inconvenient Truth*, the hard-hitting film about climate change by the former US presidential candidate Al Gore. With the help of dramatic footage and shocking statistics, he warns that humans are responsible for climate change, and unless we act now to stop it getting worse, there will be catastrophic consequences. It's a wake-up call to hear the question that will be asked of us by our children: 'Why didn't you *do* something?'

Prophets in the Bible speak in a similar way. They foretell the future, but more importantly they tell the truth – often to powerful people – about the way things are now. They warn everyone what will happen if they don't change their ways. The Bible concludes with prophecy in the book of Revelation: focusing on God's absolute power and might, it describes how he will punish the wicked and cherish the faithful.

Read Revelation 21:1-8 and compare it with 1 Samuel 2:9, 10.

The final words of verse 10 refer to 'the anointed One' – in Hebrew, 'the Messiah'. Is Hannah speaking as a thankful mother, or does she sound more like a prophet? After all, her son, Samuel, was destined to become one of Israel's great prophets.

Through modern communications media, we can hear different prophetic voices from across the world. Who do you think is telling the truth about the way things are today? Which voices are warning us about what will happen in the future?

Prayer

Father, we pray for your modern prophets who tell inconvenient truths to powerful people. Those who have ears to hear, let them hear.

23

Nurture

Home for Good is a UK charity that encourages families to provide loving homes for children in care, and encourages churches to 'wrap around' foster and adoptive families with practical love. The charity trains church leaders and workers in how to understand and respond to the particular challenges faced by looked-after children and their new families.

Read 1 Samuel 2:11-17, 22-25.

Samuel's story is the tale of a loving mother and the sacred giving of her son, but it frames a very different family history. Eli is a faithful priest whose family is totally dysfunctional. He becomes Samuel's foster father, but he is old and tired, and his own sons are running riot in the Lord's house. We can hear the weariness of a man at the end of his tether when he complains to them, 'Why do you do such things?'

Have you felt at the end of your tether with your own children, or do you know parents who are struggling? Are there families in your church who need extra support? How might you help? How might your church help? Do you consider the needs of foster and adoptive families when planning Mothering Sunday services?

Prayer

Father, we pray for all those parents who are facing difficult times with their children. Comfort them through sleepless nights and give them strength when dealing with challenging behaviour. May they know that you are with them and they are never alone.

24

Growing up

When my children were at school, we faced the annual school uniform challenge. At the end of the summer, we would find that trouser legs were two inches too short, shirts were too tight and shoes were too small. We braved queues in the shoe shops and the local hairdressers as we joined other local families in the annual ritual of fitting children out for the new school year.

Read 1 Samuel 2:18-20.

This is perhaps the aspect of Hannah's life which seems most alien to us. Even children at boarding school today have regular visits home. In cases of divorce and family breakdown, family courts prioritise children's continued access to their parents wherever possible. Imagine what it must have been like for Hannah, seeing her child grow up at yearly intervals and wondering about him every day in between. Imagine the care that she put into her annual making of the linen ephod, his priestly uniform for the temple: she must have put love into every stitch. Picture her trying to guess his measurements, especially when he turned 14 or so and really started to grow!

Do you know parents or grandparents who have little or no contact with their children or grandchildren? How might you and your church support them?

Prayer

Pray for mothers and fathers who are separated from their children, and who see them grow up at intervals. Pray for the grandparents who also suffer because of this separation. Pray for the growing children.

25
Changing

Ponyo is a magical creature who began life as a fish, the daughter of an undersea sorcerer. She develops the ability to turn into a little girl when she befriends a boy called Sosuke. This gentle fairytale from Japanese animators, Studio Ghibli, ends with a decision that Sosuke must make: can he truly love his friend, whether she is girl or fish or something in-between? He declares that he loves everything Ponyo is and could ever be. His is an elastic, resilient love that can embrace transformation: it reminds me of the sort of love that growing, changing children need from their parents.

Hannah faced a particular challenge, as she only saw her son once a year, but she still loved everything Samuel was and would become: the little child she left for the Lord, the gangly, growing boy and the spotty youth who may have been less than keen on his mother's annual hugs!

Read Hosea 11:1-4.

This is the prophet Hosea's beautiful description of God's unfailing love for his wayward people. We are God's sons and daughters, and he consistently loves all the people we become as we change throughout our lives. What different people have you already become in your life? Child, sibling, parent, colleague, friend? Have there been times when you turned away from God? What else might God be calling you to be?

Prayer

Abba, Father, Daddy, I am your child and I know you love me. Help me to become all that you want me to be.

26

Living with God

An American youth pastor recently shared a visual sermon illustration online. A clear plastic cylinder, as tall as a person, contained around 3000 yellow ping-pong balls. This represented the number of hours that parents have in a year to teach their children about Jesus. Beside it stood a small glass vase, containing around 40 balls, representing the average number of hours the church has to do the same. The pastor's conclusion was clear: the church alone does not have the responsibility for teaching children to know and love God.

Read 1 Samuel 2:21.

God is so generous that Hannah has five more children after Samuel. Meanwhile, her firstborn 'grew up in the presence of the Lord'. This has a special meaning in Samuel's case, as he grew up serving in God's temple, but Hannah's other children, too, grew up in the Lord's presence, being cared for by loving, faithful parents who observed all the duties of their faith. Samuel learnt about God in the temple, but his siblings must have learnt about God at home, from their mother and father.

Who has taught you about God? Think about who has helped nurture your faith, both inside and outside the church. If you have children at home, think about how you might get closer to God as a family.

Prayer

Father, open our hearts to meet you everywhere we go and in everyone we meet. May we know your presence in our lives. Help us to show your light to others in what we do and in who we are.

27
Hannah's faith

Near Edinburgh there is a gallery whose modern art installations are out in the countryside. One of my favourites is a field of new apple trees: next to each skinny sapling is a stout ladder, beautifully carved from oak, built to last, standing in expectation of the fruit that these trees will bear. One day, this field will be an orchard and we'll need good ladders to reach the abundant crop. These waiting ladders strike me as a symbol of hope and solid faith in the promise of harvest.

Read these verses which give us glimpses of Samuel as he grows:

1 Samuel 2:26; 3:19–4:1.

These descriptions of Samuel remind me of an apple tree that grows strongly, begins to bear good fruit and eventually feeds a whole community. Hannah knew that her son was destined for great things, and her faith is like the stout oak ladder standing by the skinny sapling. She knew that a great harvest would come, and eventually, 'the word of Samuel came to all Israel'.

In your own life, who is growing and changing before your eyes? Whose future are you watching unfold? In what ways are you supporting them? Share your hopes, fears, worries and dreams for them with God.

Prayer

Lord, you are always with us, yesterday, today and forever. Watch over those we love as they venture into their own tomorrows. May we stand by them like Hannah, in certain faith and hope.

28

Here I am

The much-loved hymn, 'I, the Lord of sea and sky', has been sung at many special services I've attended in recent years. The rousing chorus is particularly apt for those who are responding to God's call to discipleship or ordained ministry. 'Here I am!' is Samuel's prompt answer to God's call in today's story.

Read 1 Samuel 3:1-18.

This is the calling of an extraordinary prophet in the dark days when 'the word of the Lord was rare'. From the outset, Samuel tells the truth unflinchingly. His first prophecy is so dire that God himself warns it will 'make both ears of anyone who hears it tingle', and his last, made from beyond the grave, is terrible enough to fell a king (1 Samuel 28:15-20). It's easy to forget that this prophet began his truth-telling work when he was just a boy.

The theologian Anne Richards, in her book *Children in the Bible*, has concluded that not only does God heal, save and bless children, but he also calls them and commissions them, just as he calls and commissions his adult disciples. This is a challenge to churches to take children seriously, as God does. Think about how children are treated in your church. Are they like guests or members of the family? Christians-in-waiting or disciples? Kids who have trouble listening or individuals, like Samuel, capable of hearing God's call?

Prayer

Lord, open my eyes to see you at work in children and young people. Open my ears to hear what they have to tell me about you.

29

Pay it forward

The phrase 'pay it forward' may have originated with the writer Lily Hardy Hammond, who wrote, 'You don't pay love back; you pay it forward.' It has come to mean repaying a debt of gratitude not to the original giver, but through acts of unearned kindness to others. The concept has been adopted by organisations and movements for social change across the world.

Read 1 Samuel 7:2-17.

When Hannah gave Samuel to the Lord, in gratitude for his gift to her, she was in effect 'paying it forward' to God's people. After the fulfilment of God's terrible promises to Samuel about Eli and his sons, Israel suffered for 20 long years at the hands of their enemies, the Philistines. The sacred Ark of the Covenant was captured and tens of thousands died. The people's faith wavered and they turned to foreign gods for help and comfort, until at last Samuel the great prophet takes charge. God rewards his prayer and constancy, and Israel's enemies are defeated. Peace is established and Samuel, the judge, leads Israel. All this, because of one woman's gift of her son: she paid God's love forward, to the benefit of his entire people.

Think about the good things other people have done for you. How might you pay their kindness forward? Can you multiply it by doing three acts of kindness for others in response to one done for you? Can you encourage others to do the same?

Prayer

Lord, help us always to give thanks, and show us how to pay your love forward.

30
Hannah's legacy

The story feels like a folk tale: a powerful prophet who works for a jealous king is sent by God to choose a new king. A father called Jesse presents seven strapping sons, but the prophet rejects them all. 'Surely there's one more?' he says. There is. The last and least is chosen by God, and so the prophet, Samuel, anoints David as the new king.

Read Isaiah 11:1-5 and compare it with 1 Samuel 2:1-10.

King David has a special place in the history of God's people. Isaiah's prophecy links Jesse's youngest son with the Messiah, and according to the genealogy which opens Matthew's Gospel, David was the lynchpin connecting Abraham to Joseph, Mary, and Jesus. To think that Hannah's son was responsible for this great king! Look for the descriptions in Isaiah's prophecy and Hannah's song that you think sound most like Jesus. Was Hannah given a glimpse down the long years that led from her son and the king he would make, to the Messiah?

Hannah's decision to give her son to God changed the course of her people's history. Have there been momentous moments or accidental decisions in your own life that led you to where you are now? Where do you see God in the choices you made? Where else might he lead you?

Prayer

Father, thank you for Hannah and her son and the difference they made to the future of your people. Guide us now in the choices we make, and help us to trust that you will walk with us into the future.

References

7. 'The Presence' by A.E. Borthwick in St Mary's Episcopal Cathedral, Edinburgh.

13. International Day of Peace: see www.un.org/en/events/peaceday/

23. Home for Good www.homeforgood.org.uk

26. Cory Austin in *YouthMin.org: Everyday Youth Pastors* group on Facebook – accessed 1.10.18.

27. Jupiter Artland www.jupiterartland.org

28. *Children in the Bible,* Anne Richards, SPCK Publishing 2013.

29. *In the Garden of Delight,* Lily Hardy Hammond, Thomas Y. Crowell 1916.

30. The anointing of David: 1 Samuel 16:1-13.

Encountered

1501200

Claire explores the ordinary places of the Easter story in which the extraordinary events of Jesus' life, death and resurrection occurred. The five sessions and accompanying meditations will lead you to examine the reality of these places and engage with the Gospel stories in a fresh, informed and imaginative way.

Revealed

1501198

This course has six weekly sessions, taking themes from film scenes and applying them to the Bible, exploring ways in which we are revealed to ourselves and to God, and how God reveals himself to us and to the world.

www.kevinmayhew.com